Bugs That Build

Cari Jackson

mc **Marshall Cavendish**
Benchmark
New York

Marshall Cavendish Benchmark
99 White Plains Road
Tarrytown, NY 10591
www.marshallcavendish.us

Library of Congress Cataloging-in-Publication Data

Jackson, Cari.
    Bugs that build / by Cari Jackson.
    p. cm. -- (Bug alert)
    Includes bibliographical references and index.
    ISBN 978-0-7614-3191-6
1.   Insects--Juvenile literature. I. Title.
    QL467.2.J325 2009
    595.7--dc22
    008014839

The photographs in this book are used by permission and through the courtesy of:

Half Title: Jenny Waterson/Bigstockphoto

Alle/ Shutterstock: 4tr, Matsonashvili Mikhail/ Shutterstock: 5, Dr. Morley Read/ Shutterstock: 6tr, Colin & Linda McKie/ Shutterstock: 7, Leo Blanchette/ Shutterstock: 8tr, Stuart Elflett/ Shutterstock: 9, Juniors Bildarchiv/ Photolibrary: 11, Shelly A. Little: 12b, Greg McCracken/ Shutterstock: 12tr, LEEN VAN DER SLIK/ Animals Animals/ Photolibrary: 13, Oxford Scientific/ Photolibrary: 15, Oxford Scientific/ Photolibrary: 17, Joy Stein/ Shutterstock: 19, Jenny Waterson/Bigstockphoto: 20tr, David Curl / Oxford Scientific/ Photolibrary: 21, 8781118005/ Shutterstock: 22tr, Michael McCoy/ Photo Researchers/ Photolibrary: 23, Maslov Dmitry/ Shutterstock: 24tr, Charles F. Badland: 24b, Juniors Bildarchiv/ Photolibrary: 25, WebSubstance/ Istockphoto: 26tr, Robin Bush/ Oxford Scientific / Photolibrary: 27, NASA: 28, Jakez/ Shutterstock: 29.

Cover photo: : Paulo De Oliveira/ Photolibrary

Illustrators: Amit Tayal, Rishi Bhardwaj, Kusum Kala, Pooja Shukla

Illustrations: Q2AMedia Art Bank

Created by: Q2A Media

Creative Director: Simmi Sikka

Series Editor: Maura Christopher

Series Art Director: Sudakshina Basu

Series Designers: Mansi Mittal, Rati Mathur and Shruti Bahl

Photo research by Sejal Sehgal

Series Project Managers: Ravneet Kaur and Shekhar Kapur

Printed in Malaysia

1 3 5 6 4 2

Contents

Why Do Bugs Build?

Bugs build for different reasons. Many bugs, such as termites, build structures where they can lay their eggs and raise their young. Ants build chambers where they can store their food.

Take Cover!

Bugs build homes for protection from predators and bad weather. Some build homes that they carry with them. Their homes cover their bodies to protect them from being eaten. Bugs also build their homes with comfort in mind. Termites and ants build mounds that help regulate the temperature indoors.

Suppertime

Bugs also build to catch prey. Spiders weave big webs that catch flying insects. A bug called the caddisfly lives under water. Some caddisfly **larvae** spin webs to catch floating insects and plant matter.

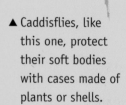

▲ Caddisflies, like this one, protect their soft bodies with cases made of plants or shells.

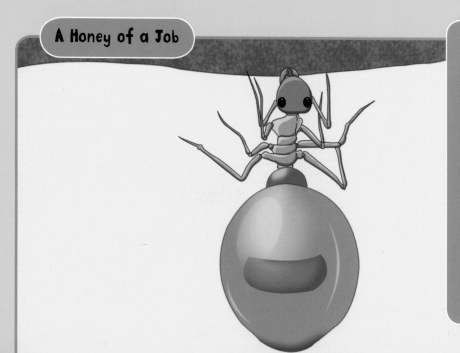

A Honey of a Job

A Job For Everyone

Social bugs work together to run their large colonies. Each member of the colony is designed to do a specific job. For instance, **worker** bees can secrete wax flakes for building the nest. Soldier termites have large heads they use to defend the nest. And the honeypot ant uses some of its workers as living honey jars. They fill their stomachs with sweet plant juices until they swell up like a balloon. Other workers collect the juice as needed.

Glands on the spider's lower abdomen secrete liquid silk proteins. The liquid meets the air and stretches into long strands. The spider has two or three spinnerets that weave the strong strands into an even stronger fiber.

When spiders sense a predator, they pump their legs to shake the web. The movement makes it difficult for predators to strike and helps to launch the spider out of the web to avoid an attack.

A bite from a golden orb weaver is painful, but not deadly.

Golden silk orb weaver spiders can weave webs more than 3 feet across, not including the support strands that stretch many more feet to nearby trees or shrubs.

What Do Bugs Build?

Bugs build amazing structures. They use dirt, wood, and substances that their bodies produce. Termites can build mounds that are taller than a house! Bees create perfect hexagonal, or six-sided, cells made of wax. Many bugs live together with thousands of others in big colonies. They need big homes.

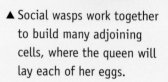

▲ Social wasps work together to build many adjoining cells, where the queen will lay each of her eggs.

Lonesome Bugs

Some bugs live almost their whole lives completely alone. They only meet another of their kind when they mate. Even when a bug lives alone, it needs protection. Potter wasps build a little home for each of its **eggs**. When the eggs hatch, they find that their mother has left them a supply of food.

Where Do Bugs Build?

Bugs build homes everywhere. Sometimes bugs share homes with us. Some wasps build nests under the eaves of our roofs. Ants dig tunnels below our lawns. Spiders build webs in trees in our yard.

Are Humans Like Bugs?

Humans build houses to be protected from storms. We have kitchens, where we cook and store our food. Our air-conditioning and heating systems cool or warm the air in our homes. We make clothes to keep us warm and protect our skin from things that can hurt us. We build nets to catch fish. As you read, think about how humans are like bugs.

Human Nests

Termites in the United States live only in wood or under the ground. Mound-building termites live in Africa, Australia, and South America.

This type of termite mound is called a cathedral mound. Different species of termites build different styles of mounds.

Termites have the largest nests of any insect. The largest termite mound, found in Australia, measured more than 20 feet across at the base.

Wasps

Social wasps, such as hornets and yellow jackets, live together in communities called colonies. A nest can hold thousands of hot-tempered wasps. Wasps fiercely defend their homes, stinging unwelcome intruders again and again.

What Do They Build?

Social wasps build paper nests. A female wasp called a **queen** starts her nest alone. Using her **mandibles**, she chews wood pulp. She stretches it into thin layers. She shapes the layers into a stem from which the nest will hang. Then she builds hexagonal cells. The pulp dries into tough paper. She lays an egg in each cell. The eggs develop into worker wasps.

Underground Hideout

Some wasps build their nests in high places. Others build in empty animal burrows in the ground. If the nest gets too big for the hole, the workers dig around the nest. They drag pebbles out of the hole. If a rock is too big, they dig under it until it sinks into the dirt.

▶ If an egg is fertilized it becomes a female. All workers are female, but only the queen can lay eggs.

Eaten Alive!

Potter wasps live alone. A female forms clay into a little pot for each of her eggs. Then she hunts for caterpillars and beetle larvae. She paralyzes her prey with her stinger and drops them into the pots. She lays an egg in each pot and secures it to the top with a sticky fiber that she produces. When the larva hatches, it eats the helpless bugs alive.

Potter Wasp Pot

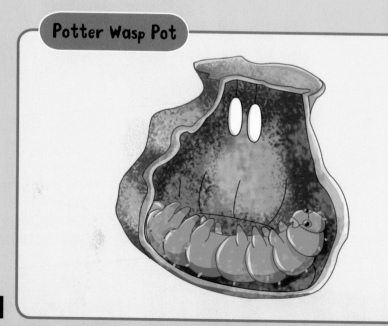

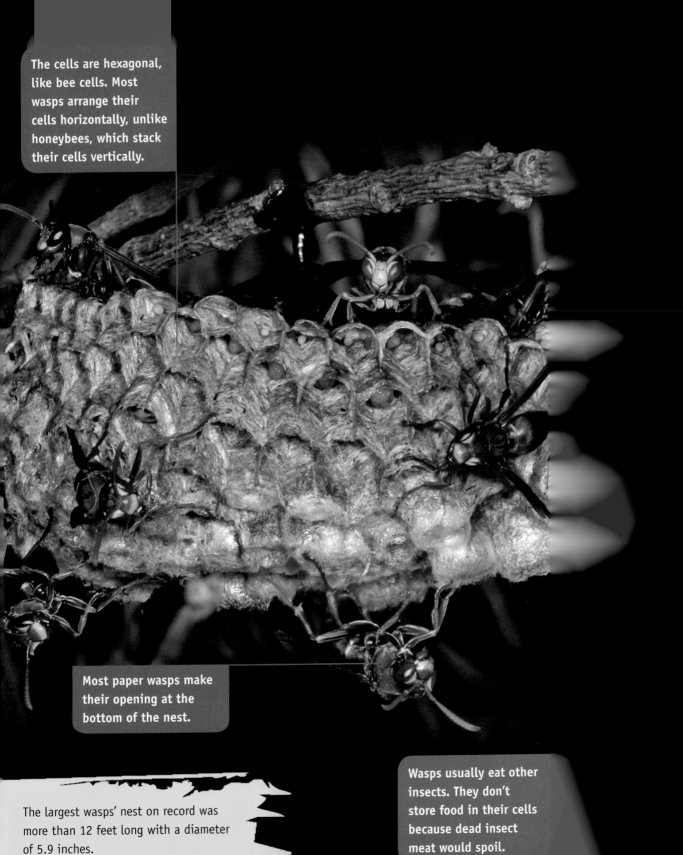

The cells are hexagonal, like bee cells. Most wasps arrange their cells horizontally, unlike honeybees, which stack their cells vertically.

Most paper wasps make their opening at the bottom of the nest.

The largest wasps' nest on record was more than 12 feet long with a diameter of 5.9 inches.

Wasps usually eat other insects. They don't store food in their cells because dead insect meat would spoil.

Bees

There are 20,000 species of bees, but honeybees are the hardest workers. If you add up the distance of all the trips honeybees take to produce a pound of honey, it would equal twice the distance around the world.

What Do They Build?

Honeybees build wax nests inside hives. Hives are natural structures or human-built boxes in which bees make their homes. Worker bees secrete, or discharge, wax flakes. They shape them into hexagonal cells that fit together. The queen lays eggs in the cells at the center. The outer cells hold **pollen** and honey to feed the bee larvae. Bees build a wall around the nest. As many as 80,000 bees live in a single colony. The queen can live for five years.

Moving House

Workers build a bigger cell and feed a larva more honey to produce a new queen. The new queen stays with the nest. The old queen leaves with a large group of workers, called a **swarm**. When they find a good spot, they start building their new home.

◄ An egg will develop into a new queen, a female worker bee, or a male **drone**. Drones mate with the queen. Afterward, female workers kill the drone or drive it out of the nest.

A Bee's Life

It takes twenty-one days for a worker bee to develop from egg to larva to pupa to adult. An adult stays the same size and lives for another six weeks. It works different jobs at different ages.

Days 1-2: Clean the nest.

Days 3-11: Feed the larvae.

Days 12-17: Build and repair the nest.

Days 18-21: Guard the nest.

Days 22-45: Collect pollen and nectar.

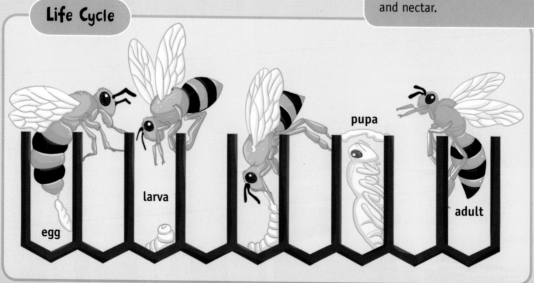

Life Cycle

egg

larva

pupa

adult

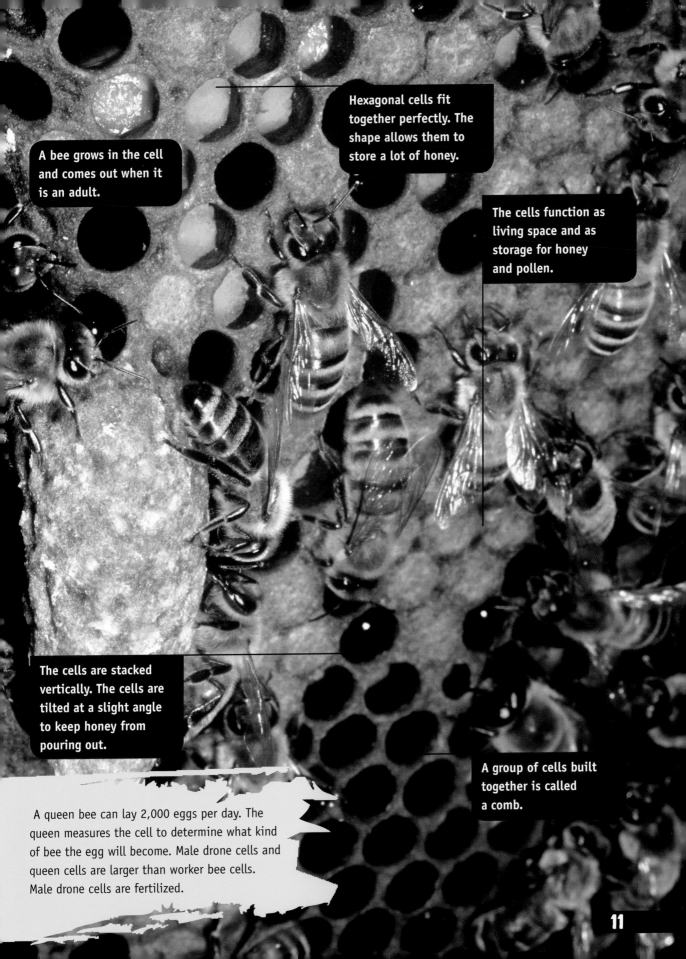

A bee grows in the cell and comes out when it is an adult.

Hexagonal cells fit together perfectly. The shape allows them to store a lot of honey.

The cells function as living space and as storage for honey and pollen.

The cells are stacked vertically. The cells are tilted at a slight angle to keep honey from pouring out.

A group of cells built together is called a comb.

A queen bee can lay 2,000 eggs per day. The queen measures the cell to determine what kind of bee the egg will become. Male drone cells and queen cells are larger than worker bee cells. Male drone cells are fertilized.

Spiders

Unlike the other bugs mentioned earlier, spiders are arachnids. They have eight legs instead of six. Many spiders make webs. The golden orb spider makes the largest and strongest web.

What Do They Build?

Golden orb spiders spin webs of gold-colored silk. The spider lets the wind carry a trail of its silk. Once the thread attaches to something, the spider walks to the middle of the strand. Then it lets another thread go. When it attaches, the web has a Y shape. The spider then weaves sticky thread around and around. It builds its web in an hour. The webs are so strong that some people use them as fishing nets!

Trapped!

The web catches flying insects for the spider to eat. Birds occasionally get themselves tangled up in spider webs, but the spider doesn't eat them. The birds ruin the web, so the spider builds barrier webs and creates lines of insect husks to warn the birds away.

▲ The golden orb spiders, from the genus *Nephila*, weave their webs more tightly than other large spiders. They catch smaller insects in their web and bite their prey to subdue them.

Spooky Trail

In 2007, a giant web covered 200 yards of a park trail in Texas. A variety of spider species cooperated in constructing the massive web. **Entomologists** think moist conditions created an abundance of mosquitoes. So the spiders, which normally eat each other when they live closely together, feasted on the mosquitoes instead. These webs are rare but show up every few years.

Monster Web

The female golden orb spider lays her eggs in a hole in the ground that she lines with silk. After the **spiderlings** hatch, they have to go off alone— spider siblings have a bad habit of eating one another!

Scientists think that the golden color of the spider silk attracts bees looking for nectar and pollen.

Bagworms

Bagworms aren't worms at all. They are the larval stage of moths in the *Psychidae* family. They can roam around, but they never leave home. Bagworms make little houses for themselves that they drag around with them.

What Do They Build?

As soon as a bagworm emerges from its egg, it spins a silk tube around its body. Then it attaches grass, sticks, or other materials to the silk. When the bagworm grows too big, it builds a new case. Some species of bagworm build messy cases. Others arrange sticks in a perfectly straight pattern. Male bagworms become moths with wings. Female bagworms never get wings.

Look Closely

The grass and stick cases **camouflage**, or hide, the slow moving bagworms. Predators have a hard time spotting them. When a bagworm senses danger, it ducks into its case and seals itself up with a silk string.

Bagworm Life Cycle

1 **Winter**
The eggs sit in a bag made by the previous year's female.

2 **Spring**
Eggs hatch. Each larva builds a case for itself with silk and plant material.

3 **Summer**
The larvae feed and **molt**, or shed old cases.

4 Then the larvae close the bag and turn upside down in the bag. They stay there for about four weeks as **pupae**.

5 **Fall**
They emerge as moths, although the female has no wings. The female attracts a mate. Then she lays her eggs in her case.

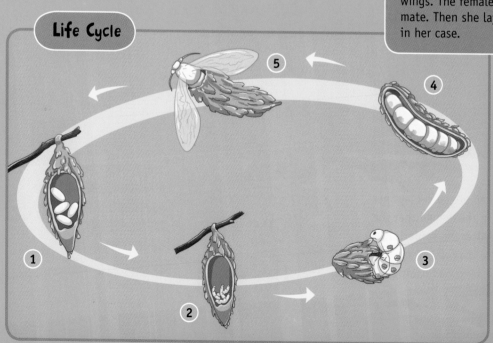

Life Cycle

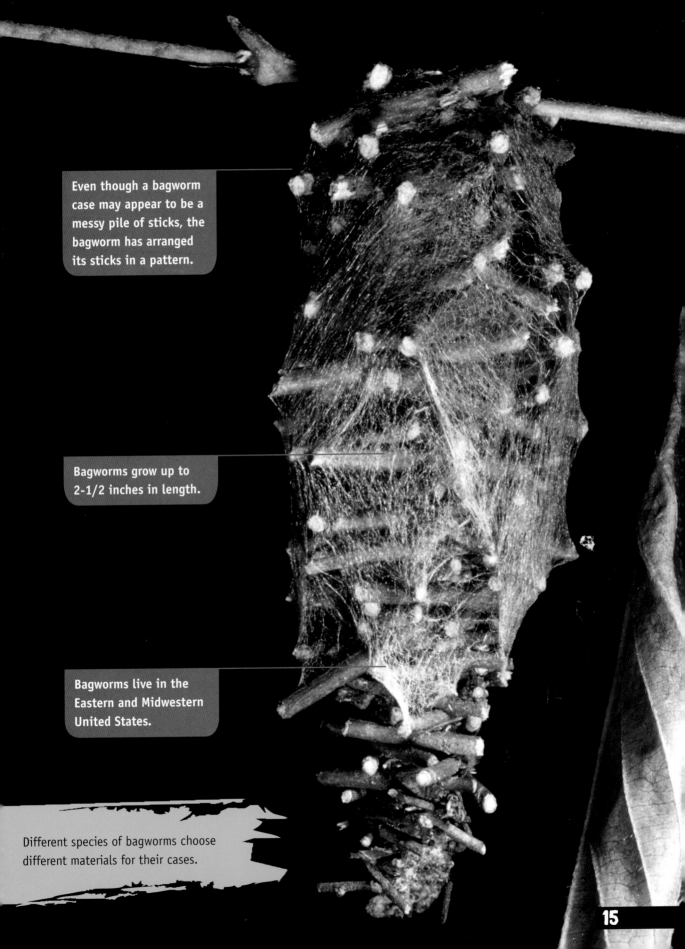

Even though a bagworm case may appear to be a messy pile of sticks, the bagworm has arranged its sticks in a pattern.

Bagworms grow up to 2-1/2 inches in length.

Bagworms live in the Eastern and Midwestern United States.

Different species of bagworms choose different materials for their cases.

Caddisflies

Caddisflies are small mothlike insects that are found all over the world. As larvae, caddisflies live underwater in lakes, ponds, and streams. These creatures move very slowly and seem to live a life of leisure.

What Do They Build?

Some caddisfly larvae build cases for themselves that are very similar to bagworm cases. Caddisfly larvae spin silk and use sand, snail shells, or bits of plants to build their protective cases. When a larva pupates, it attaches its case to something near the water's edge and closes its opening. It emerges as a moth and quickly leaves the water.

Pollution Alarm

Caddisflies breathe under water through gills. These bugs are very sensitive to water pollution. They are also an important food source for fish. When there are a lot of caddisflies living in water, it means that the underwater **ecosystem** is healthy.

Born Free

Some caddisfly larvae don't build cases. They spin funnel-shaped nets underwater and attach the net to branches or a plant. Rushing water keeps the funnel open. They sit at the bottom of the net and wait for prey to fall into the trap.

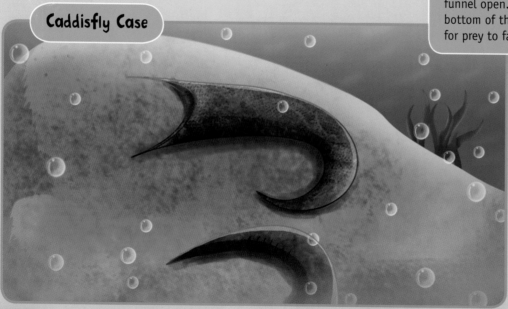

Caddisfly Case

Sometimes caddisflies attach live snails to their cases. The snail dies of starvation.

When caddisflies live in running water, they build their cases using heavier materials, such as pebbles.

Caddisflies move very slowly as they carry their case. Claws at their tail end hold onto the case.

17

Tent Caterpillars

The Eastern tent caterpillar is the larval stage of the moth *Malacosoma americanum*. They live in groups as caterpillars for four to six weeks. When a caterpillar is fully grown, it spins a cocoon for itself and pupates into a moth.

What Do They Build?

Tent caterpillars build tents. In the fall, a moth lays an egg mass of 150 to 400 eggs on a tree. The tent caterpillars hatch in early March. They work together to spin their tents in the crooks of tree branches. They expand their home each day as they grow bigger. Caterpillars leave the nest to feed in early morning, in the evening, and at night if it's not too cold.

▲ Caterpillars thrash around to ward off predators. Birds don't like to eat them because they don't like the taste.

Come and Get It!

The caterpillars trail a silk string as they march about the tree. The scent of the trail tells other caterpillars how to find a good supply of leaves. They follow the string back home when they are as full as possible.

Stop Them!

A large group of tent caterpillars can strip many trees of all leaves. The trees usually recover, but the pests can damage the tree or prevent it from growing fruit. To stop caterpillars from harming your favorite backyard tree, your family can do these things:

1. Remove the egg masses during winter.
2. Try to remove smaller nests by hand in spring.
3. Cut off any limbs where a larger nest lives.
4. Some people burn the nests, but this isn't recommended. It can damage the tree.

Tent Caterpillar

Eastern tent caterpillars love to build their nests on wild cherry, apple, and crabapple trees. In a pinch, they'll settle for hawthorn, maple, cherry, peach, pear, and plum trees.

Caterpillars gather together in a tight cluster to preserve heat.

They spin most of their silk on the side with the most light.

The silk allows light through so that the caterpillars can bask in the sun. This helps them digest their food.

Dung Beetles

Dung beetles live in dung for their whole lives. They are very important for the environment. They help soil absorb nutrients. They prevent flies from breeding in manure.

What Do They Build?

Dung beetles make homes out of dung. Dung beetles often work together in pairs consisting of a male and a female. The two beetles dig a nest under a pile of dung. They roll dung into balls and drag the balls into the burrow. Then the female lays her eggs in the dung ball, which serves as food for the larvae. When a pupa becomes an adult, it digs its way out of the ball.

Good Days

Sometimes dung beetles stop developing if there is a **drought**. They will remain as pupae and wait until the weather improves. When the weather is right, they emerge.

▲ Dung beetles have a hard outer shell and wings.

Life Cycle

1 An adult female dung beetle lays an egg in a dung ball.
2 The larva develops and feeds on the dung.
3 The larvae pupate. Sometimes they pupate for long periods.
4 The adult beetle digs its way out of the ball.
5 Male and female dung beetles sometimes work together to build a nest underground and roll dung into balls.

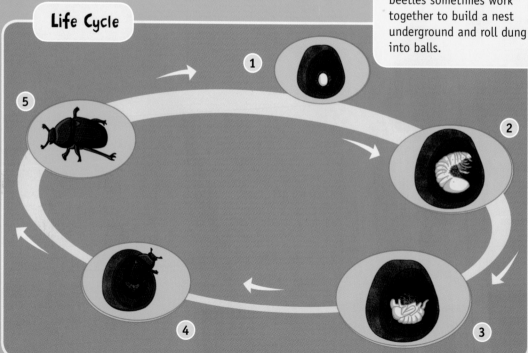

Life Cycle

The dung beetle may seem dirty, but really it helps the environment stay clean. It removes dung from above the ground and buries it below ground.

Dung beetles don't need any other food source besides dung, not even water.

Dung beetles have legs that are specialized for rolling and shoveling dung.

Flies and parasites breed in dung. With less dung surrounding them, cows have fewer flies and parasites bothering them.

Ants

There are more than 12,000 species of ants. All ants are social, like bees. Weaver ants are amazing builders and communicators. Weaver ant colonies can contain 500,000 ants, living in 150 different nests.

▲ Weaver ants live in the tropical forests of Africa, Australia and Southeast Asia.

What Do They Build?

Weaver ants use live leaves to build their nests in trees. Chains of worker ants form along the edges of two leaves. They shorten the chain one ant at a time, pulling the edges together. Each ant then holds a larva in its mandibles and gently squeezes the larva to extract silk. The ants use the silk to glue the edges of the leaves together. Scientists were surprised to discover that these ants use tools, just like humans do!

Community Helpers

Some plants, such as the hibiscus, secrete a scent to attract weaver ants. Weaver ants eat leaf-eating insects. They also have painful bites, which keeps away hungry animals. People use weaver ants as pest control in tree orchards.

Nature's Glue

1 Adult weaver ants create a chain between leaves.
2 The ants shorten the chain one ant at a time.
3 Once the leaves are close together, the adult ants carry larva to the work site.
4 The adult weaver ants do not produce silk. They use the colony's larva like a glue gun, squeezing the larva silk onto the edges of the leaves to glue the leaves together.

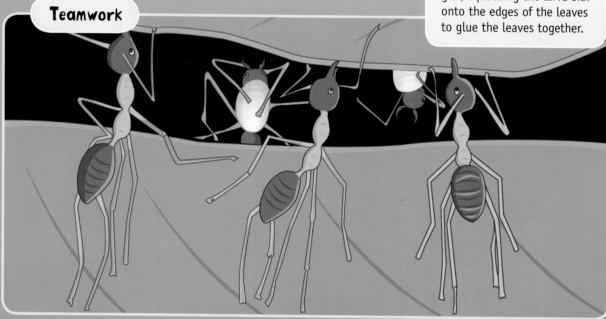

Teamwork

Weaver ants do not damage the trees that they live in. The leaves remain alive and attached to the tree as they provide a home to the ants.

A colony has one queen. The queen keeps her eggs in separate nests that hang from one tree or several nearby trees. A colony can live for about eight years.

More Ants

Many ants dig underground to make their nests. Some, such as the red wood ant, build large mounds to protect the nest below from the elements and predators. These anthills can be as large as 5 feet high. The underground tunnels descend the same distance down.

What Do They Build?

Red wood ants start building their nest underground. A queen starts the nest all by herself. She digs a little hole and blocks the entrance. Then she lays her eggs and tends to her brood for as long as a year. When the first workers emerge, they take over these tasks. They dig more tunnels. They strengthen the walls with a mortar made out of soil and secretions from their bodies.

Working Together

The ants gather pine needles, moss, and wood pieces for building the mound. If a load is heavy, other ants help out. The anthill begins to grow. Meanwhile, the queen keeps laying eggs. A colony can grow to hundreds of thousands of ants.

▲ Unlike worker bees that are all the same size, red wood ant workers come in different sizes. Smaller workers work inside the nest. Larger workers work outside.

Underground Nest

Invisible Home

How can we know what underground nests look like? Scientist Walter Tschinkel figured out a way. He poured plaster into the opening of an underground harvester ant nest. When he dug out the sculpture, it revealed the shape of the nest.

Red wood ants, also known as formica ants, live in Europe and Asia. They are considered among the most intelligent of insect species.

Ants constantly move moist pieces at the bottom of the mound to the top to dry out. Mold grows in moist environments. It can ruin a nest.

The dome shape of the mound helps to gather sunlight to warm the nest.

Ants cover any open entrances at night and when it gets cold.

The living chambers reach far into the soil below the mound.

Termites

Termites are the master builders of the insect world. The tallest termite mound ever built reached 42 feet high and was found in Africa. Some colonies house three million termites. If three million tiny termites were lined up, the column would stretch one hundred miles!

What Do They Build?

Some termites build nests that remain hidden underground. But in Africa, Asia, Australia and South America, the most skilled termite colonies build big mounds. Termites use bits of soil and wood as their main building material. They use their own droppings or spit as a hardening glue. Termite mounds are rock hard.

A Big Family

A colony's king and queen stay together in the nest for life, which can last fifty years. The queen can lay 7,000 eggs a day. The eggs hatch into soldiers, workers, or **reproductives**. The big soldiers guard the nest. The small, soft-bodied workers build, clean, gather food, and care for the young. Reproductives have wings and fly away to start new colonies.

▲ Worker termites do all the work around the nest except for guarding it, a job left to the soldier termites. Workers have to feed the soldiers, because the soldiers' heads are too large for them to feed themselves.

Without a Map

The king and queen live in the large royal cell near the center of the nest. The queen is full of eggs.

Workers carry the eggs to brood chambers near the royal cell.

Some termites farm fungi, such as mushrooms, to eat.

Termites have a natural air conditioning system. Air enters tiny holes in the walls, and then travels throughout the tunnels and chambers. Warm air rises out of the nest through the chimneys. The temperature in a nest never varies more than one degree.

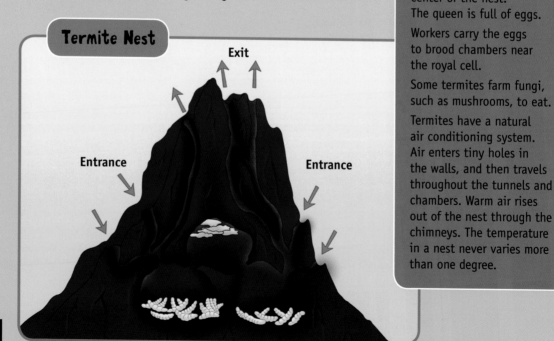

Termite Nest

Exit

Entrance

Entrance

Towers built by compass termites can be 20 feet high and 10 feet wide, but these homes are very thin.

The thin top keeps the tower from absorbing too much heat from the midday sun.

The long sides face east and west to absorb the milder heat of the rising and setting sun.

The world's tallest non-human structures are built by termites. These towers are found in Australia.

Bugs as Teachers

People can learn a lot from studying how bugs build their homes. Biomimicry **is a type of science that studies how humans can copy the way things are done in nature. What can we learn from bugs that build?**

Golden Orb Spider

Scientists study golden orb spider silk, which is the strongest natural fiber in the world. They hope to create an identical fiber to make stronger parachutes, artificial tendons, and bulletproof fabrics. Kevlar is the strongest human-made fiber, but its makers have to use dangerous sulfuric acid to create it. Synthetic, or human-made, spider silk would only need water to be created. Plants altered by humans could produce an identical fiber.

Honeybees

Bees' honeycombs provide the most support with the fewest materials. Builders use honeycomb shapes inside hollow wooden and steel structures. The structure is still strong, but it does not require as much wood or steel to create.

Termites

Heating and cooling a building uses a lot of energy. But termites achieve perfectly air-conditioned nests with no energy at all. Architects modeled a building in Harare, Zimbabwe, after termite mounds. Cold air flows through holes beneath the floor. Warm air exits the building through a chimney, much like it does in some termite mounds.

Ants

Ants have small brains, but they work together and build complex structures. Scientists at NASA study how ants communicate. NASA's newest robots will work together in large groups like ants do. One day, these robot "swarms" may build homes for astronauts on the moon or on Mars.

▼ NASA's program to produce robots that communicate with each other is called A.N.T.S., Autonomous Nano Technology Swarm.

The Credit Lyonnais tower in Lyon, France, is known for its honeycomb design.

Ancient Greeks guessed that the honeycomb shape used the fewest materials to attain the most space. It took 2,000 years, but mathematicians finally proved that theory correct in 1999 by using some heavy-duty mathematic formulas.

Bugs Data

Books

Greenaway, Theresa. *Big Book of Bugs*. New York, NY: Dorling Kindersley, 2000.

Winner, Cherie. Everything Bug: *What Kids Really Want to Know about Insects and Spiders*. Flagstaff, AZ: NorthWord Press, 2004.

Internet Sites

Visit these Web sites for more information:

Insect Lore

www.insectlore.com

Play games that make you giggle.

Insects.org

www.insects.org

Look at photos and discover more insects.

Smithsonian National Museum of Natural History

www.entomology.si.edu

Visit one of the largest online insect collections in the world.

Glossary

arachnid: A group of invertebrate creatures that have two body segments and four pairs of walking legs; arachnids include spiders, ticks, and scorpions.

biomimicry: The study of how humans can copy the way things are done in nature.

camouflage: To make something blend into its surroundings so that it is difficult to see.

colony: A large group of animals that lives together, usually under one queen or a king and queen.

drone: A male bee that has no stinger.

drought: A long period with no rain.

ecosystem: A community of different living things and the environment in which they live.

egg: The first stage of life for most animals.

entomologist: A scientists that studies insects.

larva(plural larvae): The second stage of life for most animals; some larva can live on their own, like moth larva that are caterpillars or bagworms.

mandibles: The grinding mouthparts of an insect.

molt: To shed a case or skin as something grows.

pollen: A yellow dust produced by flowers, which is necessary for plant reproduction.

pupa(plural pupae): The third stage of life for many animals; usually the insect is closed in a cocoon or case from which it will emerge as an adult.

queen: The only egg-laying female in a colony; she is tended to by workers.

reproductives: Insects whose sole purpose is to reproduce.

spiderlings: Newly hatched spiders.

swarm: A large, moving group of insects.

workers: Male or female insects that do not reproduce but perform many duties in a colony.

Index